DESIGN STYLES

Unleash your creativity and update
every room in an instant

DESIGN
STYLES

p

This is a Parragon Publishing Book
First printed in 2002

Parragon Publishing
Queen Street House
4 Queen Street
Bath BA1 1HE
United Kingdom

Created and produced by The Bridgewater Book Company Ltd, Lewes, East Sussex

Creative Director Steve Knowlden
Art Director Johnny Pau
Editorial Director Fiona Biggs
Senior Editor Mark Truman
Photographers Steve Gorton, Alistair Hughes

ISBN: 0-75258-083-3

Printed in China

Contents

Introduction

From stenciling and painting to making cabinets and soft furnishings, *Design Styles* offers a wealth of inspiring ideas to liven up your home. Whether you like small design details that can bring a touch of color and class and have a big impact on your living environment, or you want to revamp a room completely, there are projects here to suit you. Whatever your level of expertise, you can quickly and easily add color and style to your home.

ABOVE **A plain lamp base can be modified to provide an attractive detail in a room's decorative scheme or even to form the keynote of a room's style. Here the seaside is evoked through the use of shells and a wet sand look applied to the base of a table lamp.**

If you want to liven up your living room or give your bedroom decor a boost, then you need look no further than this book. There is a whole raft of simple step-by-step projects aimed at transforming your living space.

Nothing transforms an entire room quite like paint. Paint techniques that are easy to learn but bring impressive results are featured in Painter's Palette (pages 8–21). Projects here include inspiring and evocative ideas from Morocco, Africa and the Mediterranean. There is also guidance on different paint techniques and styles. You can try painting checks or blocks of color or experiment with stenciling.

Stenciling is not just confined to wall projects, however. In Floors & Walls (pages 22–33) we show you how to stencil a floor border. There are also projects on laying a floating wooden floor and ideas for making walls more interesting with tongue-and-groove paneling or cane or bamboo wall panels.

The need to screen out light and noise from a room need not mean that drapes and blinds have to be purely functional. In Window Ways (pages 34–45) we show how to make tab-head drapes and muslin no-sew drapes that are in themselves attractive features.

Revamping old furniture is a satisfying way of cheering up tired old items and saving money. In

Furniture Facelifts (pages 46–57) you will discover how to transform tables, chairs, and headboards using a variety of materials, including paint, strong utility fabric, and even mosaic tiles.

The search for sufficient storage space is a constant bugbear in the modern home. In What's in Store? (pages 58–69) we look at ways of increasing storage space in attractive and stylish ways. Whether you're considering extra shelving, making a small cabinet, or simply wanting to transform the look of your storage system, there's a project idea here for you.

Going Soft (pages 70–81) includes a raft of soft furnishings projects, from floor cushions to quilts, that will not only bring warmth and comfort but also provide accent colors and focal points to your living space.

It's the smallest design details in a house that really turn it into a home, as Little Details (pages 82–93) will demonstrate!

ABOVE **By simply removing cabinet doors from a plain base unit and using willow baskets on the shelves as pull-out drawers, you can give a room a completely new country look.**

LEFT Revamping old furniture is not only great fun, it saves money and can help to give your home a different feeling altogether. This table and chair have been renovated in a lively Provençal style to evoke the feeling of rural France.

Painter's Palette

Choosing the correct color scheme for your home is one of the most important decisions you will have to make about home decoration because it has a major impact on how you feel about your living space. You might find inspiration in the color schemes and design ideas included here from around the world, whether it's the rusty reds, earthy browns, and yellow ochers of the African landscape or the cool, chalky colors of Mediterranean homes.

Painting styles can be lively and fun, too. Consider the powerful potential of stencils—a very simple but effective means of transforming a room. Color-blocking can provide a very dramatic visual feature in a living room or hallway, and why not consider an appealing gingham wall to brighten up a nursery?

YOU WILL NEED:

- POWDER BLUE PAINT
  FOR BACKGROUND
- SAMPLE POTS OF
  TWO PINKS
- SAMPLE POT OF GREEN
- STENCIL MATERIAL
  (MYLAR OR STENCIL
  CARD IF YOU PREFER),
  OR BUY A READY-CUT
  ROSE STENCIL
- SPRAYMOUNT
- CRAFT KNIFE
- 3 STENCIL BRUSHES
- 3 WHITE SAUCERS
- PLUMB LINE
- SQUARE OF CARD
  (TO MARK DISTANCE
  BETWEEN MOTIFS).
  THE SIZE OF THE
  SQUARE DEPENDS
  ON THE SIZE OF THE
  MOTIF AND YOUR
  TASTE.

PROJECT ONE
A rose-stenciled wall

If you like pattern and have uneven walls, then stenciling is the way to go, because wallpaper requires walls that are smooth and even. This is a very romantic, feminine style for a pretty bedroom. The blue rose-patterned walls have a look of faded textiles and combine well with lace, muslin, and plenty of vintage floral fabrics used for cushions and bed covers. The walls provide a perfect backdrop for traditional bedroom furniture like dressing tables, Lloyd Loom chairs, iron bedsteads, and closets. Keep a look-out for pretty old vases, mirrors, and lamps that could be used to add authenticity to the look.

Copy this pattern or enlarge it using the grid system. The rose pattern was used here at the size of 2¹⁄₂in/60mm across. The stencil can be cut from waxed card or special stencil plastic available from craft stores.

HOW TO DO IT

Stenciling a wall pattern is quicker than putting up wallpaper and also a lot cheaper. Use the smallest amount of paint on your brush and practice on paper before you start painting the wall.

STEP 1 Make the pattern for the stencil. Coat the back of the pattern with Spraymount and stick it onto the stencil material. Use a sharp craft knife and cut out the stencil carefully.

STEP 2 Peel off the paper pattern, then spray the back of the stencil with Spraymount and leave it to become tacky.

STEP 3 Hang the plumb line 10in/250mm from one corner of the wall and position the card with the line running through two corners. Make a pencil mark at each corner, then move the card down, placing the top point on the lowest mark, and repeat to the baseboard. Mark up the whole wall in this way.

STEP 4 Position the stencil and smooth it onto the wall. Put the paints on the saucers and dab off brushes with paper towels so little remains on the brush.

STEP 5 Begin stenciling with the dark pink in the middle of the rose, then move on to the pale pink for the outer petals. Lift the stencil to check on the result as you go.

STEP 6 Use the green paint for the leaves and stem. Lift the stencil to check the result. Position it on the next mark and repeat the pattern until the wall is covered with roses.

Painting a gingham wall

YOU WILL NEED:

- SMALL FOAM ROLLER
  AND TRAY
- PAINTER'S TAPE
  1⅝IN/4CM WIDE
- CRAFT KNIFE
- WALLPAPER PASTE
- SPIRIT LEVEL
- PLUMB LINE
  (OPTIONAL)
- TEST POT OF PALE
  GREEN PAINT

Gingham is one of the freshest fabrics around and it will never, ever go out of fashion. This project shows how to customize a small foam roller and give the nursery walls a gingham effect. You can do this on a colored background if you prefer, but white is traditional and always makes a room look bigger and brighter. Most nursery borders look good with gingham, and if you buy one first you can coordinate the colors.

Gingham made easy—a simple trick with a small foam roller can transform a nursery wall, making it look bigger and brighter.

HOW TO DO IT

STEP 1 Wrap the painter's tape around the middle of the roller, dividing it into three equal parts.

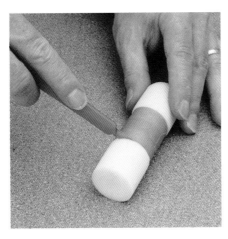

STEP 2 Cut down to the middle of the roller in a straight line following the edge of the tape. Turn the roller and cut all the way around, then once across between the lines.

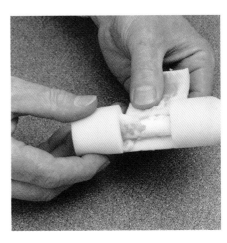

STEP 3 Peel off the painter's tape and middle foam section.

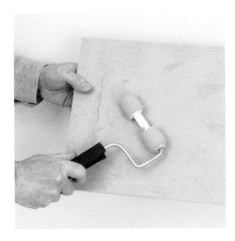

STEP 4 Mix the wallpaper paste following the instructions on the pack, and then mix it half and half with the paint in the roller tray.

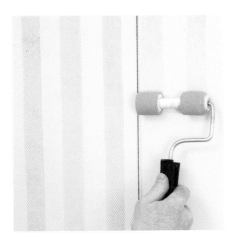

STEP 5 Hang the plumb line from the top of the wall to give you a vertical guide to follow. Run the roller through the paint/wallpaper paste mixture and begin painting in one corner, applying a medium pressure and continuing to within about 2in/5cm of the baseboard. This final bit can be filled in with the offcut from the roller. Continue in this way to complete all the vertical stripes.

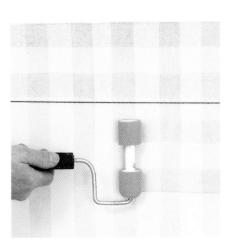

STEP 6 Place the spirit level on the wall and make some small guide marks for the first horizontal band of striping. The next stripes can be aligned with the first, but check with the level on each alternate row so that you don't drift away from the horizontal.

PROJECT THREE

Color-blocking

YOU WILL NEED:
- PAINTER'S TAPE
- PLUMB LINE
- CARPENTER'S LEVEL
- PENCIL
- MATCH POTS (LATEX, METALLICS, OR TEXTURED PAINTS)
- PAINT BRUSH
- WALLPAPER PASTE IF COLOR-WASHING

The wonderful thing about this decorating idea is that you can use test pots for all the feature colors. The base color is applied throughout the whole room, then the dining area is enlivened with blocks of color. This can be done in all sorts of ways using different colors and textures. A multicolored wall of squares or rectangles, a graduated color change from left to right, or deeper, more saturated shades of the background color are some ideas to try. Contrasts in texture are important, too, and can be introduced with metallic paints, chalky distempers or by thinning the latex paint with wallpaper paste to make a transparent glaze.

The wall of this dining area is decorated in multicolored rectangles. You could introduce contrasts in texture by using metallic, chalky, or even glazed paint.

HOW TO DO IT

STEP 1 Having decided upon the shape, size and position of the squares or rectangles on the wall, mark the verticals along the baseboard in pencil.

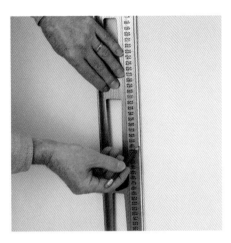

STEP 2 Hang the plumb line down the wall as a vertical guide, then use the carpenter's level and a pencil to make guide marks for the grid going up the wall.

STEP 3 Run tape up from the baseboard in straight lines. Then, using the level to check that the corners are square, run tape horizontally across the wall, intersecting the verticals and completing the grid.

STEP 4 For a color-wash effect, mix wallpaper paste into the latex (half and half) and spread the glaze with random brush strokes.

STEP 5 Apply the paints of your choice to the squares or rectangles.

STEP 6 Once the paint has dried, carefully peel off all the painter's tape.

TIP
You can use metallic paints as well, to catch the light and make the room appear larger. These are now generally available from home improvement centers.

YOU WILL NEED:

• PAINT

• PAINTER'S TAPE

• BRUSHES

• DARK WOODSTAIN

• ACCESSORIES SUCH
  AS WOVEN MATS,
  DRUMS, BEADWORK,
  GOURD BOWLS,
  SOAPSTONE
  CARVINGS, AND
  HIDE RUGS

PROJECT FOUR

The African room

The colors of Africa are drawn from the landscape: rusty reds and dark, mud browns of the earth, yellow ochers of the sun, and pale, sky blues are combined with the rich, ebony black of cooking pots on the open fire. The style is plain with organic shapes and bold patterns. Look out for woven and printed African textiles for throws and cushion covers, wood-carved figures, woven grass matting, clay pots, gourd bowls, and African recycled tin and wirework.

This African-style wall reflects the colors of the landscape—the rusty red of the earth, the soft, yellow ocher of the sun, and the blue sky between. A woven grass mat in a bold, spiral pattern completes the effect.

HOW TO DO IT

STEP 1 Measure and mark 39in/1m up the wall from the floor and stick up a line of painter's tape.

STEP 2 Paint the wall above the tape a soft, yellow ocher color. Use random brush strokes to sweep the color in different directions.

STEP 3 Paint from the floor to the tape in a rich, earthy red.

STEP 4 Remove the tape and paint a freehand brush line using a pale stone-colored or blue paint. Don't be nervous—it should look hand-painted.

STEP 5 Cover the divan with a rough-weave African cloth, tucked under tightly at the edges. Add cushions covered in dark brown and cream or indigo blue, batik-patterned cottons, or fabric patterned like zebra, giraffe or leopard skin.

STEP 6 Use grass matting on the floor, baskets woven from grasses, gourd bowls, a pendant light with an African sun hat as a shade, and a small table painted black and covered with a woven place mat.

YOU WILL NEED:

- PAINT WITH A BLUE PIGMENT
- PAINTER'S TAPE
- BRUSH
- STENCIL PAPER
- CRAFT KNIFE
- ACCESSORIES SUCH AS TOOLED LEATHER POUFFES, BEADED AND MIRRORED CUSHIONS, KAFTANS TO BE MADE INTO CUSHIONS AND ENGRAVED BRASSWARE

PROJECT FIVE

The Moroccan room

The north of Africa has an Arab culture where strong Islamic principles influence the decorative traditions. The homes have cool marble floors, arched shuttered windows, and mathematical patterns everywhere. The look is exotic, mysterious, and highly stylized. Look out for tasselled and mirrored textiles, kilim rugs, small, carved shelves, and Ali Baba pots.

This stepped, geometric-pattern border stenciled on a wall shows the mathematical patterns typical of the Moroccan decorative tradition.

HOW TO DO IT

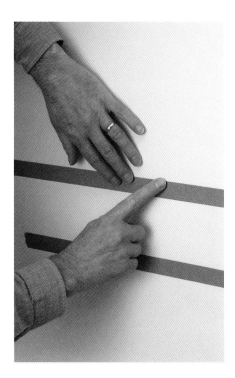

STEP 1 Mark a tile's depth white border on the wall.

STEP 2 Paint the wall above and below the border in a deep blue paint.

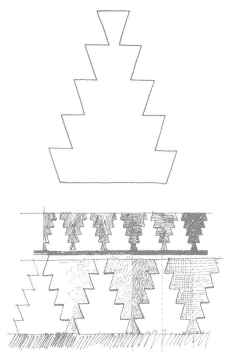

Enlarge the stencil above and transfer the pattern to plastic or stencil paper. Cut out carefully using a sharp craft knife.

STEP 3 Stencil the stepped geometric pattern in the border using the stencil pattern provided in emerald green, deep red, and black on white.

STEP 4 Lay Moroccan rugs and dhurries overlapping each other to cover the floor. Hang an arched, framed mirror, beaded bags, mirrored cloth wall hangings and small carved shelves on the wall.

STEP 5 Place a date palm in an Ali Baba pot on the floor, and a large brass tray on the small table laid with a set of Moroccan tea glasses.

YOU WILL NEED:
- PAINT
- CHAIR RAIL
- PANEL ADHESIVE
- COUNTERSUNK
  SCREWS
- STENCIL PAPER
- CRAFT KNIFE
- BRUSH
- ACCESSORIES SUCH
  AS GERANIUMS IN
  TERRA COTTA POTS,
  BRASS OIL LAMPS,
  BLUE AND WHITE
  CUSHIONS,
  PATTERNED PLATES
  AND SMALL PICTURES
  IN FRAMES

PROJECT SIX

The Mediterranean room

There are many countries and islands around the Mediterranean Sea, and each has its own distinctive decorating style. The influence of the warm, dry climate is seen in the cool interiors with tiled floors and shuttered windows. White is the dominant color, its brilliance enhanced by the azure blue sky. The dry climate simplifies the decorating because no sealants are needed. Walls are painted with chalky distemper and wood is left unvarnished. There are different traditional embroidery, weaving, ceramic, and ironwork patterns throughout the Mediterranean.

This wall has been divided using a wooden molding, painted a deep turquoise blue. The paint above and below has a chalky texture. A simple jar of wild flowers hanging from a picture hook will complete the effect.

HOW TO DO IT

STEP 1 Divide the wall at the height that a chair rail would be using a wooden molding. This can be applied with panel adhesive and strengthened with a few countersunk screws.

STEP 2 Paint the lower half of the wall using a plaster pink, chalky finish paint.

STEP 3 Paint the top half with a chalky-textured cream paint.

STEP 4 Paint the chair rail deep turquoise or cobalt blue.

STEP 5 Stencil a grapevine along the top of the wall. This does not have to look realistic in vine colors, just stencil it in one color to look like a shadow in dark green or terra cotta.

STEP 6 Cover the divan with a blue and white Greek embroidered bedspread, and hang up a Greek fisherman's lamp.

STEP 7 Hang a rustic, unvarnished wooden shelf and a group of small pictures in frames. Cover the table with a white lace-edged cloth and a vase of bright flowers. Add red geraniums in terra cotta pots, blue and white rustic ceramic wares, and a rush-seated chair.

Enlarge the stencil below and transfer the pattern to plastic or stencil paper. Cut out carefully using a craft knife.

Floors & Walls

A floor's main purpose in the home is primarily functional, and generally you will find that practicality triumphs over style and design. A floor will always need to be hard-wearing and some areas, such as hallways, more so than others, but this need not necessarily mean that it can't look great as well. Whether you want to brighten up your floor with an attractive stencil design, or add a touch of class by laying laminated flooring, there is guidance in the next few pages. Paneling can completely transform a room, whether in the form of tongue-and-groove woodwork or cane wall panels. A trip to your local garden center or hardware store could pay dividends and give your living room a new lease of life. Or why not make a screen to divide a room into two with a temporary "wall" that is stylish and practical?

YOU WILL NEED:
- 12IN/30CM X 8IN/20CM RECTANGLE CUT FROM A SHEET OF WAXED STENCIL CARD
- CRAFT KNIFE
- ADHESIVE SPRAY
- LARGE STENCIL BRUSH
- TWO WHITE PLATES
- ABSORBENT PAPER TOWEL
- PAINT IN TWO CONTRASTING COLORS (EITHER LATEX AND VARNISH, OR A PREPARATORY FLOOR PAINT)
- CLEAR, STRONG POLYURETHANE VARNISH (OPTIONAL)
- BRUSH TO APPLY THE VARNISH
- MINERAL SPIRITS TO CLEAN THE BRUSH

PROJECT ONE

Stenciling a floor border

Stenciling on the floor is really easy, and you never get the problem of paint running as sometimes happens on walls. For this project you need a 12in/30cm x 8in/20cm rectangle cut out of stencil card. You can then design and cut out your own stencil pattern to form a border around the edge of the room. This could be done on vinyl floor tiles with special vinyl paint, or using a latex paint with a varnish to seal it on wood.

You could paint a solid background color, or alternate two colors which can then be reversed for the pattern.

A stencil pattern border can brighten up either a wooden or a vinyl floor. For vinyl, use a special vinyl paint. Use a few repetitive patterns for a balanced, geometric effect.

HOW TO DO IT

STEP 1 Photocopy or redraw the pattern so that it fills most of the stencil card—leave a ¾– 1³⁄₈in/2–3cm border around the edges so that the stencil is not too flimsy. Spray the back of the pattern with adhesive spray and stick it firmly to the card.

STEP 2 Use a craft knife to cut out the stencil carefully. Always cut outwards from the corners, and try to cut curves with one even movement to avoid jagged edges.

STEP 3 Spray the back of the stencil with adhesive spray and leave for 5 minutes. Put a blob of each color on the plates. You need a very small amount of paint for stenciling. Coat the brush with paint, and then dab most of it off on the paper towel.

STEP 4 Mark the guidelines in chalk if you are painting onto wooden floorboards. Place the stencil on the floor and smooth it flat. Apply the first color.

STEP 5 Apply the second color in exactly the same way.

STEP 6 If you are painting a wooden floor with latex, apply 1–3 coats of varnish when the paint is bone dry. Floor paint is tough enough not to need varnish.

Photocopy or redraw this pattern on stencil card.

PROJECT TWO

Laying a floating wooden floor

Laminated flooring is a fashion that's here to stay. It's easy to lay, looks a million dollars, and is really easy to keep clean. It's made in average floorboard widths and comes in a wide range of stained hardwood veneers, varying between ⅜in/10mm and ¾in/19mm in depth. The best are unsurprisingly the most expensive. Laminates are stain-resistant, won't splinter, and because of their tongue-and-groove fitting, you avoid drafts coming up through gaps in the floorboards.

Existing floors need to be leveled before you begin. Concrete floors will need a heavy-duty PVC damp-proof membrane, and all floors need a good underlay of either ⁵⁄₁₆in/7mm felt boards, or ⅛in/2mm foam sheeting. When you buy laminated flooring you will also need a fitting kit and laminated flooring adhesive. The kit will contain full fitting instructions and spacers to be inserted between the floor and the baseboard (the floor will expand after it has been laid).

Laminated flooring is stain-resistant, splinter- and draught-free. It comes in a range of stained veneers, the best of which are the most expensive.

HOW TO DO IT

STEP 1 Put down the underlay, butting the joints together.

STEP 2 Lay the first board with the groove on the edge next to the wall. Place spacers at the end and along the wall.

STEP 3 Lay another board loosely (without glue) at the end of the first, engaging the tongue and groove. Add another board or, depending upon the space, cut one to fit the remaining space, allowing enough room for a spacer next to the wall. Use a string line to check that the boards are straight, otherwise the other boards will be out of line as well.

STEP 4 Run a continuous line of adhesive along the tongue and groove.

STEP 5 Use the tamping block with a hammer to force the boards tightly together.

STEP 6 Immediately wipe off the excess glue, which will ooze out between the joints, with a damp cloth. Begin the second row with the off-cut from the first, providing it is at least 12in/30cm long. Lay the first three rows, and leave the adhesive to dry before you continue. The last row of boards may have to be cut across its width to fit into the space, and you must remember to allow for the spacers. Finally, remove the spacers and fit the quarter-round molding to the baseboard to cover the expansion gap.

YOU WILL NEED:

- TONGUE-AND-GROOVE PANELING TO FIT AROUND THE WALLS (MEASURE AND BUY PANELING KITS TO FIT THE LENGTH REQUIRED)
- THREE LENGTHS OF 1 x ½IN/25 x 12MM BATTENS FOR EACH WALL LENGTH
- SHELF 3 x 1IN/ 75 x 25MM DAR SOFTWOOD TO FIT AROUND THE ROOM (MEASURE THE LENGTH REQUIRED)
- SUPPORT BRACKETS FOR THE SHELF TO BE SPACED 24IN/60CM APART
- ¼IN/6MM WALL ANCHORS
- BOX OF No. 6, 2IN/50MM SCREWS
- BOX OF 1IN/25MM BRADS
- SMALL HAMMER
- DRILL WITH ¼IN/6MM AND ³/₃₂IN/2MM PILOT BITS
- FINE CENTER PUNCH
- MITER SAW OR BLOCK WITH BACKSAW
- SCREWDRIVER
- LONG RULE WITH CARPENTER'S LEVEL
- PENCIL

PROJECT THREE

Lining the walls with tongue-and-groove paneling

This is a lovely style for a bathroom that can be given a country or seaside accent, depending upon the color and paint finish used. You may even like the idea of staining the wood dark brown to give it a distinctly masculine style. The shelf around the top of the paneling can have hooks screwed into it for hanging up small hand towels and flannels.

Wooden paneling can be customized to the style you want by the choice of paint color—blues and greens for a seaside theme, or earth browns and creams for a country feel. Dark-brown wood stain will give it a masculine style.

HOW TO DO IT

STEP 1 Use the rule with the carpenter's level to mark three positions for the battening on the wall to align with the top, middle and bottom of the panels.

STEP 2 Drill and insert wall anchors spaced 20in/50cm apart, and then screw the battens onto the wall. Beginning in one corner, place the end plank against the wall and check the vertical with the carpenter's level. Hammer a brad through the inside edge of the tongue angled slightly inward. Do this into all three battens. Drive the brad head below the surface.

STEP 3 Fit the groove of the next plank into the tongue of the first. To ensure a tight fit, place a spare piece of wood along the edge and tap it with the hammer. Continue in the same way to complete the paneling. Planks will almost certainly need to be cut down to fit at the corners. Draw a line where this is required, clamp the plank in the jaws of a workbench and cut with a backsaw or powersaw.

STEP 4 Use a center punch to knock the brad heads into the lumber.

STEP 5 Cut the shelf planks to fit the wall lengths, mitering the ends for a neat fit in the corners and at any joins. Check and mark the shelf position on the wall with a carpenter's level. Drill pilot holes in the planks and the panels for the brackets.

STEP 6 Screw the brackets into the front of the paneling and down through the shelf into the top of the brackets. Prime and paint with enamel paint, or use latex sealed with marine-quality varnish.

PROJECT FOUR

Cane or bamboo wall panels

YOU WILL NEED:

- SPLIT CANE OR
  BAMBOO PANELS
  TO FIT THE LENGTH
  OF A WALL
- MOLDING TO FINISH
  OFF EDGES OF THE
  PANELS TO FIT THE
  LENGTH OF THE WALL
- DRILL AND FINE
  DRILL BITS
- LONG RULE WITH
  A CARPENTER'S LEVEL
- STAPLE GUN
- BRADS
- SMALL HAMMER

One of the hottest new looks around is applied texture, especially using natural material to line interior walls. Cane and bamboo are both ideal materials for this kind of home decoration project.

The garden center is the best place to look for cane or bamboo paneling; it is sold in a range of heights and lengths and is not expensive. Other options for this kind of project include willow and reed panels.

You could fix the panels to wall cleats that can be easily removed or, as has been done here, use a staple gun and brads to attach the panels to the wall.

Add accessories in natural materials for a totally organic look.

HOW TO DO IT

Bamboo or cane panels are not expensive but will quite easily transform a room. Before you start this project, paint any areas of the wall that are not going to be covered with bamboo or cane.

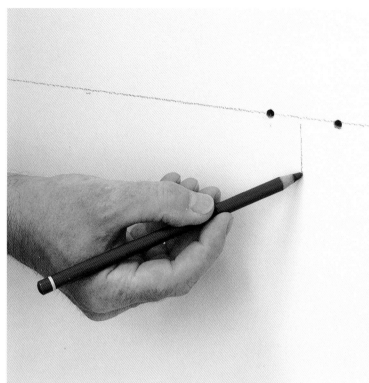

STEP 1 Measure and cut the required lengths of bamboo or cane. Use the fine drill bit to find the positions of the studs in the wall.

STEP 2 Mark the positions on the wall above the height of the panels so they can be found once the panels are in place.

STEP 3 Smooth the panel up against the wall and use a staple gun or brads to fix it to the studs in the wall.

STEP 4 Fix the moldings along the top and bottom of the panels with brads and a small hammer.

YOU WILL NEED:
- FABRIC
- 2OZ/56G WADDING
- SCREEN
- SCISSORS
- SPRAY ADHESIVE
- T-PINS
- STAPLE GUN
- BRAID

PROJECT FIVE

Screens

Not surprisingly, screens are enjoying a renewed popularity. They add a regal touch to a room and can hide clutter or divide a room, concealing gym equipment or a home office. Plain wooden screens, available ready to be painted or covered in your choice of fabric, come with different shaped tops.

Old screens can be found at secondhand shops and if they are scruffy and battered, covering them with a smart fabric will make them look brand new and disguise imperfections. Alternatively, a carpenter could make one to your specifications.

Most fabrics are suitable. Sheer fabrics need to be mounted on a plain, closely woven fabric and treated as one thickness if covering a solid screen. If you wish to use a luxurious but expensive fabric, use it on the side of the screen that faces into a room, with a cheaper coordinating fabric on the other side. Extra fabric will be needed to match printed patterns across the screen.

A screen with frames instead of solid panels can have tension wires strung across and sheer fabric panels suspended between them. Alternatively, lightweight fabric panels can be attached to the upper and lower frame with touch-and-close tape.

If you are re-covering an old screen, remove any old fabric covering and trimmings. Lever out tin tacks: if any are impossible to remove, hammer them into the screen so they do not snag you or the fabric. Separate the screen panels by unscrewing the hinges.

Give careful thought to the positioning of printed fabrics. If the screen is to stand with one panel more prominent than the others, place the main pattern on the prominent panel. Lay the screen panels side by side flat on the floor and lay the fabric on top. Tuck the edges under the panels. Try different arrangements to see what looks best: centering the design is the obvious choice, but try placing it off-center as an alternative.

Screens can add a touch of elegance to a room as well as being practical room dividers.

HOW TO DO IT

This screen is slightly padded with wadding on one side, but you could pad both sides if you prefer.

STEP 1 Cut 2oz/56g wadding 1in/25mm larger on all edges than each screen panel. Use a spray adhesive especially recommended for upholstery to stick the wadding to the screen panels. Cut away the excess wadding.

STEP 2 Cut the fabric for each panel front, adding 1¼in/32mm to all edges. Press the fabric and lay the first piece centrally on the panel. Pin to the wadding with T-pins. Fold the fabric smoothly over the side edges. Use a staple gun to fix the fabric in place, working outwards from the center.

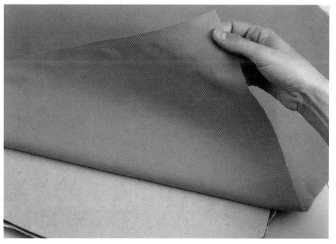

STEP 3 Smooth the fabric along the length of the panel and over the upper and lower edges, folding under the fullness neatly at the corners. Staple in place then trim away the excess fabric just inside the edges of the screen.

STEP 4 Turn the panel over and cover the other side in the same way, positioning the staples between the first row. Trim away the excess fabric as before. Starting on the lower edge, use fabric glue to stick braid that is the width of the panel on the edges. Cover the remaining panels. Join the panels with hinges.

Window Ways

Windows are quite often a main feature of a room and it is
vital to pay them the same attention you would to your selection of
furniture and fixtures and fittings. Choice of window covering can set
the tone of the whole room, for example, you may select flowing,
exotic muslin or tab-topped sheer voile.
You could also decorate the window features, such as the valance,
in a way that combines your personal taste with the theme of
a room decor. In this chapter we look at how you could bring
a Romany style to your living room through the addition of a stylishly
painted valance that you can make easily from scratch.
We also suggest a way of avoiding the use of drapes or blinds for
small bathroom windows. Simply decorate the windowpane itself
with etching spray in a way that guarantees both privacy
and an attractive window feature in your home.

YOU WILL NEED:
• VOILE
• DUPION SILK
• SCISSORS
• TAPE MEASURE
• DRAPE POLE

PROJECT ONE
Tab-top drapes

Drapes hung by tabs are very popular because, as well as being easy to make, they show off the wonderful choice of drape poles available today. Most fabrics are suitable, but smooth, lightweight or slippery fabrics are easier to draw along the pole.

These drapes are made from sheer voile, allowing the light to filter through.

HOW TO DO IT

STEP 1 To calculate fabric quantities, measure the window width and double the measurement, adding 1¼in/32mm for both side hems. Measure the intended drape drop from 2½in/63mm below the drape pole to allow for the tabs. Add 1¾in/45mm to the drop measurement for the hem and seam allowance.

STEP 2 Work out how many tabs will fit across the top of the drape. The tabs are 4¾–6in/120–150mm apart and 1¼in/32mm wide. Measure the circumference of the pole, and add 5¾in/145mm. Cut the tabs 3¼in/83mm wide (*see below*). A 2in/50mm wide strip of dupion silk the width of the drape plus 1¼in/32mm is needed for the upper band. Dupion silk is usually only 3ft/915mm wide, so it may be economical to join the band rather than cut it in a single length. Stitch a ⅜in/10mm seam allowance.

STEP 3 Cut out the drape from voile. Press ¼in/6mm under then ⅜in/10mm on the side edges. Stitch close to the inner edges. Press ⅜in/10mm under then 1in/25mm on the lower edge. Stitch close to the inner edges.

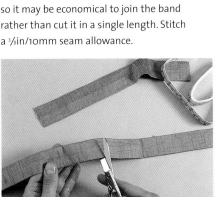

STEP 4 Cut an 3¼in/83mm wide strip of dupion silk long enough to cut the number of tabs needed. Fold lengthways in half with right sides facing. Stitch the long edges. Press the seam open. Turn right side out with a bodkin and press, placing the seam centrally. Cut into equal lengths for the tabs.

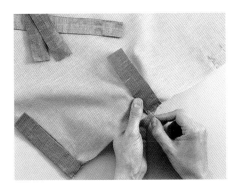

STEP 5 Fold each tab in half with the seam inside. Pin the tabs to the upper edge on the wrong side of the drape, positioning one tab at each end and spacing the rest an equal distance apart.

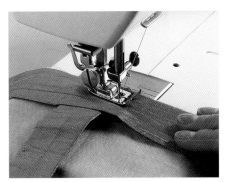

STEP 6 Cut a 2in/50mm wide strip of dupion silk for the upper band, the width of the drape plus 1¼in/32mm. Press ⅜in/10mm under on one long edge. With the right side of the band facing the wrong side of the drape, pin and stitch the band to the upper edge, with ⅜in/10mm extending beyond the sides of the drape.

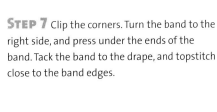

STEP 7 Clip the corners. Turn the band to the right side, and press under the ends of the band. Tack the band to the drape, and topstitch close to the band edges.

TIP
Plastic tab-top gliders are available to fit under the tabs, to help them glide along the pole.

YOU WILL NEED:
- IRON
- IRONING BOARD
- SCISSORS
- TAPE MEASURE
- STRAIGHT EDGE
- 1IN/25MM WIDTH BONDING TAPE
- CURTAIN-WIDTH MUSLIN (5FT/1.5M PREFERABLE)
- 20IN/500MM OF SAME WIDTH GRAY LINEN OR FINE COTTON LAWN
- DRAPE POLE
- POLE SUPPORTS

PROJECT TWO

Muslin no-sew drapes

Butter muslin is soft and not too transparent. It filters the light and obscures the view both into and out of a room. The unbleached cream fabric has just enough weave to be interesting, and lets in just enough light to show this off. Muslin is a very lightweight fabric and as such is ideal to use with bonding tape and an iron. The curtains are hung from a pole threaded through a fold-over casing at the top and finished with a binding hem of dove-gray linen, which adds just the right amount of weight to ensure that the drapes hang well.

No-sew muslin drapes can be made very quickly and the finish is often neater than stitching.

HOW TO DO IT

Take time to measure and turn the hems evenly and avoid touching the bonding tape with the iron.

STEP 1 Measure the window. The drapes should not be too full, so allow the width plus half again to give a slightly gathered look. Measure the length from the pole to the floor and add 4in/100mm for the fold-over casing. At the bottom, the raw edge will be enclosed in the band of linen. Place the drape lengths on the ironing board and press a folded ³⁄₄in/20mm hem.

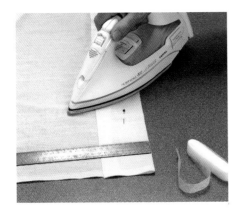

STEP 2 Draw a line 3¹⁄₄in/80mm from the first fold. Iron the bonding tape on the line. Peel off the backing and fold the top section over. Press to bond the two sides together.

STEP 3 Cut out the gray binding strips, turn over and press a small seam to fold in the raw edges.

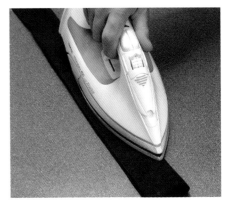

STEP 4 Place a strip of bonding tape along each of the folded seams and press with an iron to bond. Now fold them in half lengthways and press along the fold.

STEP 5 Place the raw bottom edges of the muslin inside the folded linen edgings. Pin them in place. Peel off the backing, one side at a time, and iron to bond the fabrics.

STEP 6 Press the drape lengths and feed them onto the pole.

YOU WILL NEED:
• WINDOW CLEANER
• PAPER TOWEL
• THIN PAPER
• SCISSORS
• ADHESIVE SPRAY
• ETCHING SPRAY

PROJECT THREE

Decorating a window with an etched pattern

If you have a small bathroom or very little natural light coming in, it is a shame to block the window with drapes or blinds. And when bathrooms are fitted with thick obscuring glass designed to stop the neighbors seeing you in the bath, this is not always very attractive. In both cases, and with plain glass, the window can be decorated with etching spray. This will allow you to keep clear glass in the top half of the window and stencil a frosted pattern of your own creation on the lower section, to give you all the privacy you need.

A window decorated with etching spray is a subtle and attractive way to create privacy without blocking out the light with drapes or blinds.

HOW TO DO IT

STEP 1 Clean the window and let it dry. Fold four strips of paper 1⅛in/30mm wide and the width and height of the window into a concertina, then cut out a fancy pattern on one edge. Flatten the strips out and lightly apply adhesive spray to one side.

STEP 2 Fold another three strips of paper into 1⅛in/30mm squares concertina-wise, and draw simple motifs in the middle. Cut these out and spray one side lightly, as above.

STEP 3 Stick the borders around the window up to the desired height, and then arrange the motifs across the window pane in a geometric or random pattern. Mask out the surrounding area with paper to protect it from the spray.

STEP 4 Spray on a light and even coating of etching spray. You can always apply a second coat if this is too thin and patchy, but it is best to apply one continuous coat first and then leave it to dry. Peel off one of the motifs to check the effect, and apply a second coat of etching spray if necessary.

YOU WILL NEED:
• DE-GREASING
  WINDOW CLEANING
  SPRAY AND CLOTH
• ETCHING SPRAY
• PAINTER'S TAPE
• TAPE MEASURE
  OR RULE
• PLAIN PAPER
• ADHESIVE SPRAY

PROJECT FOUR

Decorating a window with etching spray

This gives a cool, contemporary look to a bathroom window, and obscures the view from outside. The design is more of a style statement, and the spray could also be used to make a matching border for a bathroom mirror. It is a good idea to make sure you clean the window and allow it to dry completely before you start this project.

Decorating a window with etching spray adds a cool, contemporary look to your bathroom. Your own design would do just as well as the one shown.

HOW TO DO IT

STEP 1 Run a frame of painter's tape 3/4in/20mm inside the edge of the window, attaching paper to protect the area around it.

STEP 2 Enlarge the "h_2o" on a photocopier to fill an A4 sheet, then cut them out and apply adhesive spray to the back. Place the letters inside the masked frame, and then frost the window with the etching spray. Peel off the tape and the templates.

YOU WILL NEED:

• A LENGTH OF 6IN X
  1IN/150MM x 25MM
  SHELVING PLANK
  (MEASURE THE
  WIDTH OF THE
  WINDOW PLUS
  4IN/100MM)

• SHELF BRACKETS

• CARPENTER'S LEVEL

• DRILL

• MASONRY BIT AND
  WALL ANCHORS

• SCREWS FOR THE
  BRACKETS

• A LENGTH OF
  HARDBOARD
  6IN WIDE/150MM—
  ENOUGH FOR BOXING
  IN THE TWO ENDS
  AND THE LENGTH OF
  THE FRONT

• HARDBOARD PINS

• SMALL HAMMER

• WHITE CHALK PENCIL

• BLACK BASECOAT
  PLUS A SELECTION OF
  ACRYLIC COLORS

• SMALL DECORATOR'S
  BRUSH

• ARTIST'S LINING
  (LONG-HAIRED) PAINT
  BRUSHES
  (FINE, MEDIUM,
  AND BROAD)

• DRAPE ROD AND
  2 END FITTINGS

PROJECT FIVE

A painted wooden valance

A valance like this will look best fitted above a medium- to small-sized window. It is really easy to make, being basically a shelf on brackets with a strip of hardboard pinned onto the front and sides.

Valances are not very fashionable at the moment, but do suit a folksy, traditional room style, and the combination of valance and drapes makes a particularly bold Romany-style statement.

One other bonus of making a valance is that it creates another shelf in the kitchen and provides a perfect place to display painted plates, jugs, or even a vase of flowers.

A hand-painted valance sets the tone for a room's decorating style and will be much admired.

The patterns below are the outline shapes for the freehand painting. Either practice by copying them freehand or enlarge the patterns to the desired size and trace their outlines onto the pelmet. Do this by rubbing the back with chalk or using a chalk transfer paper.

HOW TO DO IT

Make a simple valance out of hardboard, paint it black, and cover it with colorful Romany patterns.

STEP 1 Mark the valance position 2in/50mm above the window recess. Check that it is straight using the carpenter's level, and draw a pencil line. Mark the screw positions for the shelf brackets on the wall and on the shelf plank.

STEP 2 Drill all the necessary holes, insert wall anchors, and fix the brackets to the wall.

STEP 3 Cut the end pieces from the length of hardboard, fix to the main length of hardboard, and then apply the basecoat. Leave to dry, then apply a second coat.

STEP 4 Roughly mark out the pattern with the chalk pencil. Avoid using a ruler—use strips of paper as measuring guides where you need them.

STEP 5 Practice the base patterns on paper first, and when your hand has loosened up move on to paint the pattern details.

STEP 6 Paint as much decoration as you like, then fix the hardboard to the shelf front and sides. Screw the rod fittings into the inside ends. Use a small brush to touch up any pinheads or exposed edges, then fix the valance to the brackets.

Furniture Facelifts

Revamping a piece of long-forgotten furniture that you have rediscovered in your loft or jumped on at the flea market is one of the most rewarding aspects of home decorating. Not only will it cost less than buying new furniture, it will provide a satisfying glow as the item is transformed using your decoration skills. These skills can range from simple painting expertise to rudimentary mosaic making. The best part about renovating old pieces of furniture is not giving the items a new lease of life—valuable though that undoubtedly is—but rather the opportunity it gives you to express your creativity and develop your burgeoning home improvement talents.

In this chapter we look at how you can brighten up tables, chairs, and headboards using a wide array of materials, including paint, varnish, fabric, and even mosaic tiles! Once you have mastered the basic skills you can improvise. Let your imagination go to work.

YOU WILL NEED:

• A PINE TABLE

• A WOODEN KITCHEN
  CHAIR

• SANDPAPER

• HOUSEHOLD BLEACH

• SCRUBBING BRUSH

• PROTECTIVE GOGGLES

• RUBBER GLOVES

• YELLOW PAINT

• PATTERN FOR CHAIR-
  BACK DRAWN ON
  TRANSFER PAPER

• PENCIL

• TUBES OF PALE AND
  DEEP BLUE PAINT FOR
  DETAIL (ACRYLIC)

• HOUSEHOLD PAINT
  BRUSH (2IN/50MM)

• ARTIST'S PAINT
  BRUSHES (ONE
  MEDIUM AND
  ONE FINE)

PROJECT ONE
A painted kitchen table and chair

Preparing meals and eating together form a central part of the Provençal lifestyle, with the kitchen table at the heart of everything. For this project a plain pine table is given a new, more decorative French style with a scrubbed top and painted legs, and the wooden kitchen chair has been given a new coat of bright yellow paint and the finishing touch of a typical French Provençal motif.

Some peeling paint or chipped enamelware is part of this look, and will give the room a sense of history.

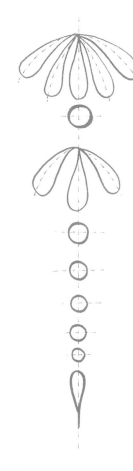

Look out for a country-style kitchen chair with a shapely backrest and, if you're very lucky, a rush seat.

Trace this pattern twice to use across the back of a chair with an extra dot between them. Chalky-backed transfer paper is ideal for this task and can be bought from art stores.

HOW TO DO IT
Give a pine table some character with a scrubbed top and brightly painted legs and paint a wooden chair to match.

STEP 1 Prepare the table legs and the chair for painting by sanding away any loose paint or varnish. Sand the top to remove all traces of varnish, then scrub it thoroughly, first with water, then with a 50/50 solution of bleach and water. Wear goggles and rubber gloves, if necessary.

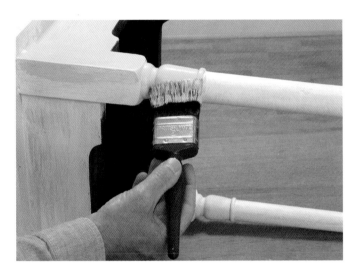

STEP 2 Apply a coat of primer, then two coats of yellow paint to the table legs and top rails.

STEP 3 Prime the chair, then apply two coats of yellow paint. Latex is used here for a mat finish, but gloss could be used instead for an easy-clean surface.

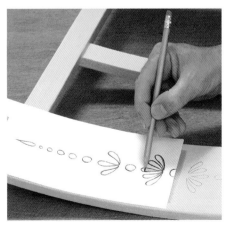

STEP 4 Trace the pattern twice to make a symmetrical pattern for the chair-back. Insert transfer paper between pattern and chair.

STEP 5 Tape the transfer paper and the pattern onto the chair-back. Go over the pattern in pencil.

STEP 6 Paint the pattern on the chair-back using free-flowing brushstrokes and two different sized brushes.

YOU WILL NEED:

- SHEET OF 1IN/25MM MDF
- PVA
- PAINT BRUSH
- DEEP RED-BROWN VINYL SILK AS THE BASE COLOR
- SMALL FOAM ROLLER AND TRAY
- WATER-BASED CLEAR GLAZE
- TUBE OF BLACK ACRYLIC PAINT TO TINT THE GLAZE (OR BLACK INK)
- 1IN/25MM BRUSH
- RUBBER OR PLASTIC GRAINING ROLLER
- SOFT COTTON CLOTH
- PLASTIC CONTAINER FOR THE GLAZE
- CLEAR MAT VARNISH

PROJECT TWO

Rosewood-graining an MDF table top

Rosewood has a deep red base with a dramatic near-black grain. The real thing is very expensive, but it is actually quite easy to fake with the aid of a rubber graining roller. This can be bought in specialized paint stores and even some hardware chainstores. MDF is an ideal material for this treatment because it has a perfectly smooth surface with no grain of its own. Buy a sheet of 1in/25mm MDF cut to a size that will suit your room and the number of people you need to seat, and support it on saw horses. If you have never tried woodgraining before, don't be put off, because it is not as technical as it appears. You will need to practice with the graining tool and glaze, however, before you paint the table. You will soon discover the right amount of glaze needed and the technique for rocking the roller as you go.

This rosewood-effect dining table has been made using a sheet of MDF, a rubber graining roller, and a deep-red vinyl silk paint.

HOW TO DO IT

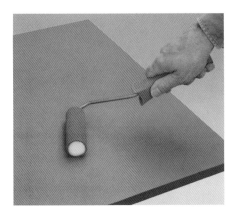

STEP 1 Paint the table top and edges with a coat of diluted PVA, 3 parts glue to 1 part water, to seal the surface.

STEP 2 Apply a coat of the red base color and leave it to dry. Check for coverage and, if it needs one, apply a second base coat.

STEP 3 Mix up the glaze using 4 parts glaze to 1 part black paint.

STEP 4 Paint the glaze over the red base coat using a flat-ended paint brush. Gently wipe the cotton cloth over the wet surface so that only the thinnest layer of glaze remains. Don't scrub it all off, and leave a fine film of glaze for the graining.

STEP 6 Do the edges of the table top in exactly the same way. Leave the graining to dry, and then apply two coats of clear mat varnish.

STEP 5 Hold the graining roller with the ridges curving down. Beginning at one end, hold the roller on the glazed surface and gently pull it toward you, rolling it over as you go.

Having reached the extremity, begin rocking it back the other way, still pulling it toward you. Continue to the end and begin again alongside the first strip.

YOU WILL NEED:
- FABRIC
- SCISSORS
- TAPE MEASURE
- IRON
- PINKING SHEARS

PROJECT THREE

Tailored dining-chair cover

A set of good-quality chairs is an important furniture investment. If you want to ring the changes, but avoid splashing out on new seating, make smart covers for a set of chairs that you have already or for a single chair that has become shabby or needs updating.

HOW TO DO IT

Choose a washable fabric to keep your chair covers looking fresh. You could also make matching napkins for a coordinated look.

STEP 1 Cut a rectangle of fabric for the inner back that is the height of the inner back plus the depth of the back plus 2in/50mm by the width of the inner back plus twice the depth of the back plus 2in/50mm. Cut a rectangle of fabric for the seat that is the seat depth plus 2in/50mm by the seat width plus 2in/50mm. Matching the centers and with the right sides facing, pin the lower edge of the inner back to the back edge of the seat, taking a 1in/25mm seam allowance.

STEP 2 With the wrong sides facing outward, place the inner back and seat on the chair. Fold the corners of the upper edge of the inner back diagonally with the right sides facing. Pin the fabric neatly along the corners of the chair. For the front skirt, cut a square or rectangle of fabric that is the front width plus 2in/50mm by the seat height plus 2¹/₂in/63mm. With the right sides facing, pin the front skirt to the front edge of the seat.

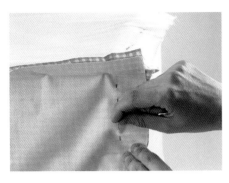

STEP 3 Cut two squares/rectangles of fabric for the side skirts (side width measurement plus 2in/50mm by the seat height plus 2½in/63mm). Right sides facing, pin side skirts to side edges of the seat. Snip the seam allowance on the inner back so it lays smoothly around the depth of the back. Pin side skirts to the inner back and side edges of side skirts and front skirt together.

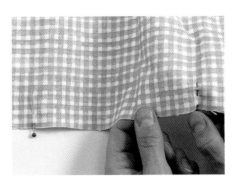

STEP 4 For the outer back, cut a rectangle of fabric that is the outer back height plus 2½in/63mm by the back width plus 14½in/368mm. Mark the top and lower edge with a pin at the center and 6¼in/163mm each side of the center for the pleat.

STEP 5 With the right side face up, bring the outer pins to the center of the fabric to form an inverted pleat. Press the pleat and tack across the upper edge.

STEP 6 With the wrong side facing outward, pin the outer back to the inner back and side skirts, repinning the fit where necessary. Using tailor's chalk, carefully mark all the seam lines where they are pinned and where the seams intersect.

STEP 7 Mark the position on the pleat where the tie fastening is to be. Unpin the outer back and skirts. On the right side of the back, work a 1in/25mm long buttonhole ¾in/20mm in from the pressed edges of the pleat at the tie position on both edges of the pleat where they meet.

STEP 8 With right sides facing, stitch the corner seams of the inner back as far as the outer back intersections. Pin and stitch the inner back to the seat (start and end at side intersections). Check fit. Trim seam allowance to ⅝in/15mm. Press the seams open.

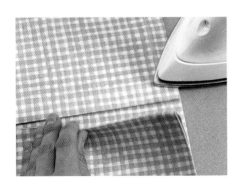

STEP 9 With the right sides facing, stitch the front skirt between the side skirts, starting at the seat intersections. Stitch the skirts to the inner back and seat, pivoting the seam at the front corners of the seat.

STEP 10 Pin and stitch the outer back to the inner back and side skirts, pivoting the seam at the upper corners. Slip the cover onto the chair and pin up the hem. Remove the cover and trim the hem to 1¼in/32mm. Press ⅜in/10mm under then ¾in/20mm on the lower edge, and stitch close to the inner pressed edge. Re-press the pleat at the lower edge.

STEP 11 Make a pattern from paper for the tie (see diagram). Cut the tie from fabric. Fold lengthways in half with right sides facing. Stitch the outer edges, taking a ⅜in/10mm seam allowance and leaving an opening to turn. Clip the corners and turn right side out. Press then slipstitch the opening closed. Insert the tie through the buttonholes and tie together.

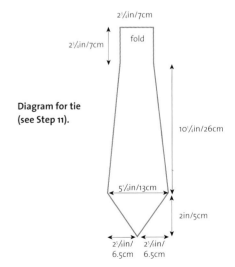

Diagram for tie (see Step 11).

2¾in/7cm
2¾in/7cm
fold
10¼in/26cm
5⅛in/13cm
2in/5cm
2⅝in/6.5cm
2⅝in/6.5cm

YOU WILL NEED:

- ALUMINUM OXIDE
- SANDING BLOCK
- T-SQUARE
- PENCIL
- TILES
- HAMMER
- WOOD GLUE
- RULER
- RAGS AND CLOTHS
- MOLDING PINS
- COUNTERPUNCH
- SPACKLING
  COMPOUND
- TILE ADHESIVE
- GROUT SPREADER
- WOODWASH
- CLEAR VARNISH
- LATEX PAINT

PROJECT FOUR

Table mosaic decoration

A battered old wooden occasional table can be given a new lease of life with a mosaic top made from cracked tiles. On this octagonal table, the mosaic pattern is defined by a softwood frame, and this technique would work well on a square or rectangular table, too.

HOW TO DO IT

STEP 1 Rub down the table top with a sheet of aluminum oxide wrapped around a cork sanding block to provide a "key."

STEP 2 Draw guidelines for the wood pieces, using a soft yellow pencil so that they can be clearly seen.

RIGHT: On this table, the cross shape is tiled with different shades of blue mosaic, which match the color of the table and contrast with the pale blue color-wash of the softwood.

STEP 3 Wrap each tile in a cloth and break it into small pieces with a hammer.

STEP 4 Check the design to make sure there are enough pieces of the right colors.

STEP 5 Miter all the wood pieces, then glue and pin them to the table, following the guidelines.

STEP 6 Spread the adhesive ⅛in/3mm deep with a ribbed spreader.

STEP 7 Position the tile pieces in the adhesive.

STEP 8 Once the adhesive has set, grout between the tile pieces.

STEP 9 Polish the mosaic. Paint and varnish the rest of the table.

YOU WILL NEED:

FOR THE STAPLED
    COVER:
• TAPE MEASURE
• FABRIC
• T-PINS
• SCISSORS
• STAPLE GUN

FOR THE SLIP-OVER
    COVER:
• TAPE MEASURE
• FABRIC
• 2oz/56G WADDING
• LINING MATERIAL
• SCISSORS
• WIDE RIBBON
• TACKS AND PINS
• NEEDLE AND
    THREAD

PROJECT FIVE

Upholstered headboards

Fabric-covered headboards give a neat finishing touch to a bed, and are comfortable to rest against if they are padded. A wooden headboard can be transformed by having a layer of foam glued to the front which is then covered with fabric, which can be stapled to it. Readymade headboards can be covered with your choice of fabric. Alternatively, make a slip-over cover that fastens around the existing headboard with ties at the sides and can be removed for laundering. A row of laced eyelets could be used instead.

Stapling fabric to a headboard can transform the bedroom by adding color and interest.

HOW TO DO IT: STAPLED COVER

This cover is quick and simple to make so you can transform your headboard in next to no time.

STEP 1 Measure the height, width, and depth of the headboard. Cut fabric that is the height plus twice the depth plus 2¼in/56mm by the width plus twice the depth plus 2¼in/56mm. Lay the headboard face up and place the fabric on top, centering any design motifs. Pin the fabric in place with T-pins.

STEP 2 Turn the headboard over and fold the fabric to the underside. Working outward from the center on the upper edge and sides, use a staple gun to staple the fabric to the back of the headboard. Neatly fold under any fullness at the curves and corners and staple in place. Staple the fabric to the back of the headboard at the lower edge. If necessary, snip the fabric to lie smoothly around the supports.

HOW TO DO IT: SLIP-OVER COVER

This cover may be easily removed for washing if need be.

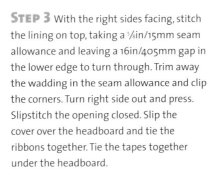

STEP 1 Measure the height, depth, and width of the headboard. Cut one rectangle of fabric, 2oz/56g wadding and lining that is twice the height plus the depth plus 1½in/38mm by the width plus the depth plus 1½in/38mm. Cut eight 18in/460mm lengths of 1½in/38mm wide ribbon for the side ties. Tack each ribbon to the side edges 5¼in/132mm and 22¼in/566mm from the lower and upper edges. Cut the extending ends in chevrons.

STEP 2 Cut four 14in/355mm lengths of ½in/12mm wide seam tape. Pin and tack to the upper and lower edges 8⅜in/215mm in from the side edges. Pin the fabric right side up on the wadding, smoothing the fabric outward from the center.

STEP 3 With the right sides facing, stitch the lining on top, taking a ⅝in/15mm seam allowance and leaving a 16in/405mm gap in the lower edge to turn through. Trim away the wadding in the seam allowance and clip the corners. Turn right side out and press. Slipstitch the opening closed. Slip the cover over the headboard and tie the ribbons together. Tie the tapes together under the headboard.

What's in Store?

Finding sufficient storage space is one of the major bugbears of the modern home. In this chapter we look at ways of maximizing your storage space as well as providing stylish and attractive alternative storage ideas. It is possible to add to a room's decorative theme with clever use of storage space. By removing the doors of a base unit or kitchen cabinet and inserting willow baskets on the shelves as pull-out drawers, for example, you can give a drab kitchen a country look. We also show you how to make a handy kitchen stool that not only acts as a seat but also provides a useful storage box in its base, and explain how you can take an existing free-standing unit and turn it into a tented closet with very little effort, thereby hiding the items formerly on display and creating an appealing feature.

YOU WILL NEED:
- SCREWDRIVER
- SPACKLING COMPOUND
- MOLDING
- MITERING SAW (OR TENON SAW AND MITERING BLOCK)
- MEDIUM-GRADE SANDPAPER
- CONTACT ADHESIVE
- MOLDING PINS
- SMALL HAMMER
- CENTER PUNCH
- ALL-PURPOSE PRIMER
- PAINT (IN A SUITABLE COUNTRY COLOR)
- SMALL FOAM PAINT ROLLER AND TRAY
- WILLOW BASKETS

PROJECT ONE

Removing cabinet doors and adding willow baskets

Any base unit or kitchen cupboard can be given a real country look by removing the doors, and using willow baskets on the shelves as pull-out drawers. In fact, it may require a leap of the imagination to convert a standard beige melamine cupboard into something beautiful, but it can be done! All you need do is whip off the doors, fill the holes and pop in the baskets, but a few trimmings will make all the difference.

A melamine cupboard can be painted after suitable priming, and the facing edges of the cupboard can be covered with a wooden moulding. They come in a range of styles, from twisted rope and oak leaves to simple half-moon and square edge. The inside of the cupboard will look good painted in a contrasting colour to the outside, and there is also the option of adding a curtain on a simple net wire. Checked gingham or even linen tea towel curtains look a million times better than old melamine, and they can be tied back to reveal the baskets inside.

Willow baskets as sliding, pull-out shelves transform standard melamine cabinets. Paint the insides and outsides of the cabinet first, and add wooden molding to the facing edges.

HOW TO DO IT

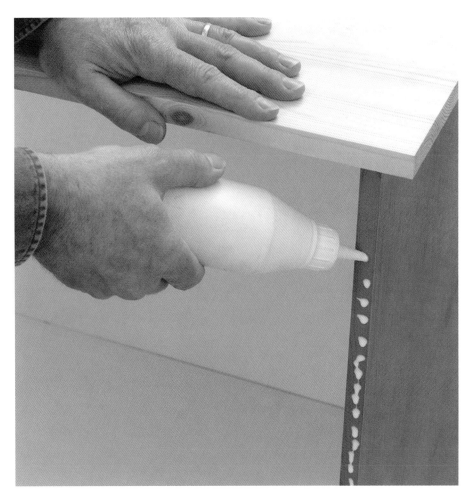

STEP 1 Unscrew the existing doors and remove the fittings. Fill the holes with spackling compound, so that the compound stands slightly proud of the surface. Once it has dried, sand the compound level.

STEP 2 Measure the frame, then cut the molding to fit, mitering the corners. Apply contact adhesive to the frame.

BASKET HANDLE IDEAS
You can use any of the following:
• Cardboard parcel labels tied on with string
• Checked ribbons
• Stitched tubes of fabric
• Threaded beads or buttons on twists of wire
• Rope loops
• Buckled leather straps

STEP 3 Stick the molding down and then add a few pins along each length. Tap the pinheads into the molding with a center punch, fill the holes, and sand smooth.

STEP 4 Prime the cabinet, and then paint it inside and out. If you are using two different colors, paint the inside of the cabinet first and let it dry before painting the area where the colors meet.

STEP 5 Buy willow baskets to fill the space across the width, leaving just enough room for them to slide easily in and out. Many baskets have handles attached, but if not there are plenty of ways to make your own.

PROJECT TWO
Stools for storage

YOU WILL NEED:

• LUMBER AS FOLLOWS
4 LEGS 2IN X 2IN/
50MM X 50MM,
23IN/58CM LONG;
4 FEET 1⅝IN/40MM
WOODEN KNOBS
WITH SCREWS;
1 BOX BASE ½IN/
12MM MDF,
12 X 12IN/30 X 30CM;
2 BOX SIDES
½IN/12MM MDF,
12 X 8IN/30 X 20CM;
2 BOX SIDES
½IN/12MM MDF,
13 X 8IN/32.5 X 20CM;
2 SEAT FRAMES
½IN/12MM MDF,
12 X 31½IN/30 X
80CM;
2 SEAT FRAMES
½IN/12MM MDF,
13 X 31½IN/
32.5 X 80CM;
1 SEAT 1IN/25MM
MDF, 14IN X 14IN/
35CM X 35CM

• PENCIL
• TAPE MEASURE
• STRAIGHT EDGE
• SAW
• WOOD GLUE
• SPACKLING
COMPOUND
• DRILL WITH
1⅝IN/2MM BIT AND
COUNTERSUNK BIT
• BOX OF 1⅝IN/40MM
No. 6 SCREWS
• PRIMER
• PAINT
• SMALL FOAM ROLLER
AND TRAY

R emember the space rule and don't waste an inch of it. This high stool is easy for a beginner to make, and has a useful storage box in the base. The stool can be painted to match the kitchen if you want it to blend in, or try primary colours with black legs for a 'Bauhaus' look.

Not an inch is wasted by this high stool, which has a storage box in the base. Experiment with colors that either match or contrast with the rest of the kitchen.

HOW TO DO IT

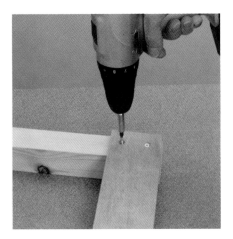

STEP 1 Make up the two shorter sides. Drill, countersink, glue, and screw the 12in/30cm seat frame across the top of each pair of legs. Check that the legs are square to the seat before fixing.

STEP 2 Drill, countersink, glue, and screw the 12in/30cm box sides at the other end to overlap the ends of the legs by ½in/12mm and allow for the depth of the box base. Check that everything is square!

STEP 3 Join the two sides of the stool by fixing the 13in/32.5cm seat frames and box sides between them.

STEP 4 Fix the base by screwing up into the legs from below. If this is a nice tight fit it will add stability. Fix the seat on from the top.

STEP 5 Fill all the countersunk holes with spackling compound, leave to set, and then sand smooth. Prime and paint the stool using a small foam roller.

STEP 6 Drill four pilot holes, then screw the wooden feet into the base.

TIPS
You might need to plane a small amount of wood from the underneath of each of the wooden knobs that are to be used as feet. Check how the stool stands on the floor and adjust the feet accordingly.

YOU WILL NEED:

• LUMBER (SEE
  LUMBER
  REQUIREMENTS,
  RIGHT) PLUS SMALL
  SCRAP OF WOOD TO
  MAKE A CATCH
• 4 HINGES
• BOLT
• SMALL BRADS
• WOOD GLUE
• HAMMER
• HANDSAW
• SCREWDRIVER
• SMALL SCREWS
• AWL
• 6 CUP HOOKS
• 2 MIRROR FIXINGS
• RUST RED PAINT
• PAINT BRUSH

PROJECT THREE
A small shuttered wall cabinet

This shallow cabinet looks like the sort of wooden shuttered window you would find in a farmhouse. Recycled timber gives the most rustic effect—or use part of a louvered door.

The idea is to make a box with a decorative lid to hang on the wall. For the backing plate, use lumber thick enough to allow for hooks to be screwed in. The traditional colors used for shuttered windows are red-brown or blue-green, both of which will soon fade and mellow in the bright sunshine to produce an attractive, weathered effect.

Hanging on the wall in an entrance hall, this key cupboard creates the illusion of a window.

Draw a template based on these designs. The cabinet made here is 11¼in/290mm x 12¾in/330mm x 1in/25mm, but adapt your template to the size you require.

LUMBER REQUIREMENTS

back: 11½in x 13in/290mm x 330mm

sides: 2 x 1in x 1in/25mm x 25mm, measuring 11½in/290mm

top/bottom: 2 x 1in x 1in/25mm x 25mm, measuring 11¼in/285mm

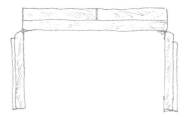

doors: 5½in x 12½in/140mm x 325mm

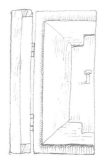

paneling:
2¾in/70mm wide x 11½in/290mm long mitered;
2¾in/70mm wide x 4⅞in/125mm long mitered

HOW TO DO IT

This idea can be adapted to suit your needs or the lumber you have available. The cabinet is simply glued and pinned together.

STEP 1 Cut all the pieces to size (*see* Lumber Requirements, opposite). Sand as necessary.

STEP 2 Make up the shallow box with simple butt joints, using wood glue and brads to secure the sides and fix them to the back.

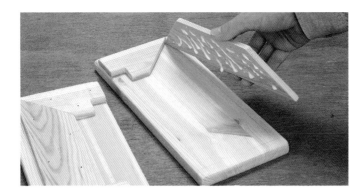

STEP 3 Make up the two front doors, adding extra panels and cross bars to give the shutter style (if required).

STEP 4 Attach the doors to the box base using two hinges for each door.

STEP 5 Fix the bolt onto the front to joint the doors in the middle.

STEP 6 Apply two coats of paint. When the cabinet is dry, screw six hooks (or more) into the back of it, then fit the mirror fixings onto the back, and fix the cabinet onto the wall.

YOU WILL NEED:

- FLOATING SHELF KIT—INCLUDING SPECIAL FITTINGS, SCREWS, AND WALL ANCHORS
- TAPE MEASURE/LONG RULER
- CARPENTER'S LEVEL
- PENCIL
- DRILL AND THE CORRECT DRILL BIT FOR YOUR WALL, I.E. MASONRY OR PLASTERBOARD

PROJECT FOUR

Floating shelves

The essence of this style is that rooms should appear to be more empty than they actually are. Create the impression of open space by fitting shelving that seems to float in the air without any visible support system.

There are several different systems on the market that work very efficiently, so instead of "re-inventing the wheel" the project shows how to use one of the existing designs. The shelves come in a range of sizes, the one used here being the shortest. Choose a length to suit the proportions of your walls and the things you wish to display, because it is important to keep to the open uncluttered style.

A few simple treasures displayed on a floating shelf look very effective.

HOW TO DO IT

Simple to fit and a minimalist's
dream, these shelves are magical.
But, as with most tricks, the
explanation is quite simple.

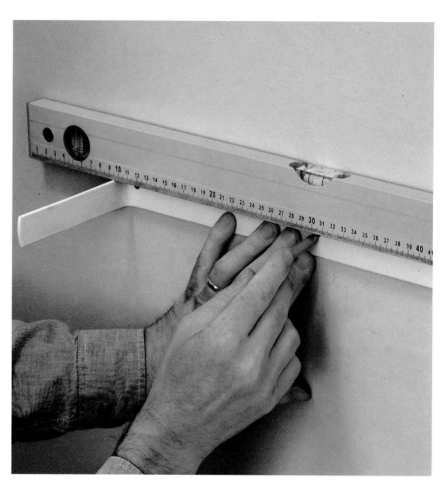

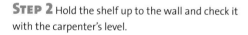

STEP 1 Having decided on the best position
for the shelf, measure and mark it on the wall
lightly in pencil.

STEP 2 Hold the shelf up to the wall and check it
with the carpenter's level.

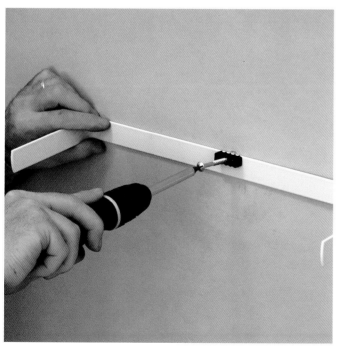

STEP 3 Mark the fixing positions for the supports, then remove them
and drill and plug the wall with anchors.

STEP 4 Fix the shelf onto the wall supports.

YOU WILL NEED:
- WOODEN STORAGE UNIT
- FABRIC
- TAPE MEASURE
- SCISSORS
- 2 BUTTONS
- 2 TOUCH-AND-FASTEN DISCS
- GLUE

PROJECT FIVE

Tented closets

Freestanding wooden units are very cheap and are great for storage purposes. The only drawbacks are that they are usually unattractive to look at and everything in them is on display.

You can solve these problems quite easily by making a streamlined fabric cover to hide the unit's contents which rolls up and fastens with buttons to give access inside the unit.

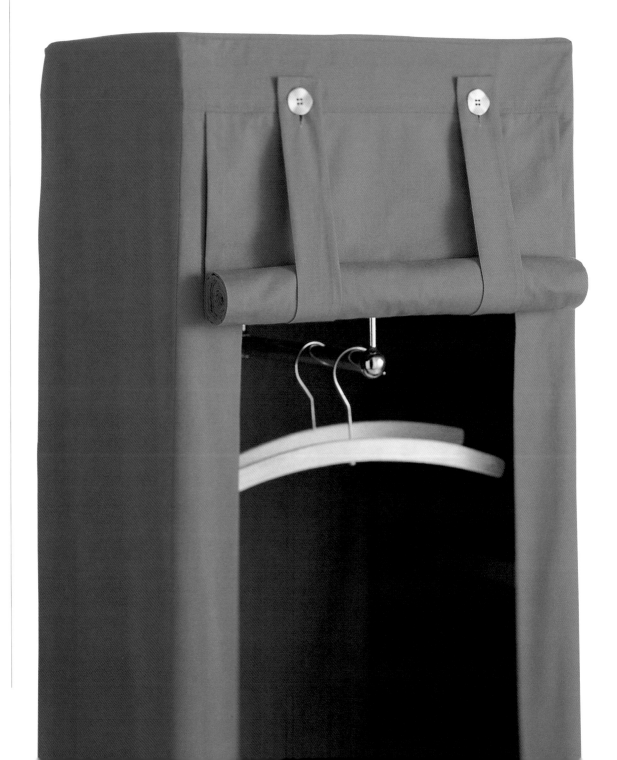

Tented closets are fun and practical. Use the same pattern to cover a wooden bookshelf and hide clutter away from view.

HOW TO DO IT

STEP 1 Measure the width, depth, and height of the unit. For the door, cut two rectangles of fabric the height of the unit minus 1½in/4cm by the width of the unit. With right sides facing, stitch together along the sides and lower edge. Clip the corners and turn right side out. Press and pin the upper raw edges together. Take a ⅝in/15mm seam allowance throughout.

STEP 2 Cut two strips of fabric 18 x 4¾in/45 x 12cm for the straps. With right sides facing, fold the straps lengthways in half, and stitch down the long edges and across one end. Clip the corners, turn right side out, and press.

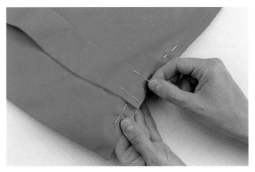

STEP 3 Work a buttonhole to fit your buttons ⅝in/1.5cm from the finished ends. Pin and tack each strap to the upper raw edge of the underside of the door 2¾in/7cm in from the side edges.

STEP 4 Cut two strips of fabric for the pediment that are the unit width plus 1¼in/3cm by 4in/10cm. With right sides facing, pin the upper edge of the door centrally to a long edge of one pediment.

STEP 5 For the front borders, cut two 6¾in/17cm wide strips of fabric that are the height of the unit minus ¾in/2cm. Press the borders lengthways in half with the wrong sides facing. Pin and tack the long raw edges together.

STEP 6 Matching the raw edges, pin the upper border edges borders to the pediment, overlapping the edges of the door. Tack the rest of the pediment on top, sandwiching door, straps and borders. Stitch the upper edge. Turn right side out and press. Tack the raw edges together. Topstitch close to the seam, then ¼in/5mm from the first stitching.

STEP 7 Cut a rectangle of fabric for the sides and back, which is the height of the unit plus 2in/5cm, by the width and twice the depth plus 1¼in/3cm. Join fabric widths if necessary with a flat felled seam. With right sides facing, stitch the front borders and ends of the pediment to the height edges, starting ⅝in/1.5cm below the upper edge. Press the seam open and neaten the edges with a zigzag stitch.

STEP 8 Cut a square/rectangle for the roof that measures the width plus 1¼in/3cm by the depth plus 1¼in/3cm. With right sides facing, pin the roof to the upper edge of the unit cover, matching pediment to width edges. Stitch, pivoting the fabric at the corners.

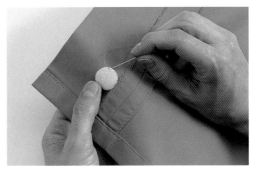

STEP 9 Turn right side out and slip the cover over the unit. Pin up a double hem. Remove the cover and sew a touch-and-fasten disc to the lower edge inside the front borders. Glue corresponding discs to lower edge of unit. Roll up door. Sew buttons to pediment.

Going Soft

Soft furnishings add texture, color, and home comforts to your living space in the form of drapes, cushions, and covers. You can choose fabrics to reflect your personality, such as fun faux fur for cushions or the subtle, sensuousness of sheer fabrics for drapes.

Whatever types you choose, you can use the colors to match in with your general room scheme or to contrast with it. Cushions, particularly, can provide a splash of color in an otherwise neutrally decorated room. But soft furnishings also have a practical function; for example, floor cushions can help to soften a room's hard edges and provide a comfortable seat. Another sitting-down opportunity is provided by the Cube Seat in this chapter—not only is it practical but it will also provide a talking point in any living room!

YOU WILL NEED:

- A FOAM/FEATHER OR
  POLYSTYRENE BEAD
  FLOOR-CUSHION PAD
  (LOW BUDGET
  SUGGESTION: BUY A
  CHEAP FLOOR CUSHION
  AND RE-COVER IT, OR
  MAKE A CALICO LINER
  AND FILL IT WITH A
  PAIR OF OLD PILLOWS)
- A CREAMY WHITE COT
  BLANKET OR 1 YARD/
  1 METER FLEECE FABRIC
- SCISSORS
- SEWING MACHINE
- IRON
- CLOTH
- BEIGE TAPESTRY WOOL
  AND A LARGE NEEDLE
  FOR FINISHING IN
  BLANKET STITCH
- WHITE THREAD

PROJECT ONE

Floor cushion

When you combine a white floor cushion with a white rug, the floor becomes very much a part of the decorating scheme. Floor cushions are comfortable for lazing about on the floor. The project is simple and relies upon finding an interesting textured fabric and a trimming. The cushion cover in the project can be made from a cot blanket, which is the perfect shape as well as being wonderfully soft and inviting, or use one yard/one meter of fleece fabric. The cover is made in the most basic way, being machined on three sides and slip-stitched closed with the cushion pad inside. The blanket stitching suits the material perfectly.

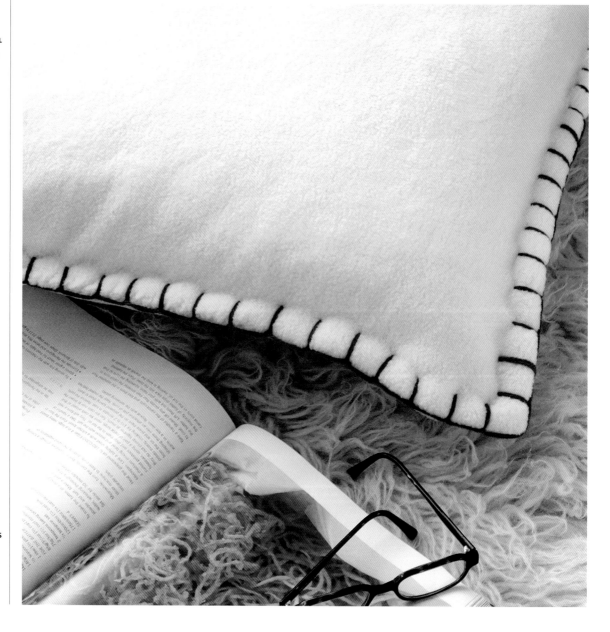

Careful combinations of textures mean that a white decoration scheme can still be warm and welcoming.

HOW TO DO IT

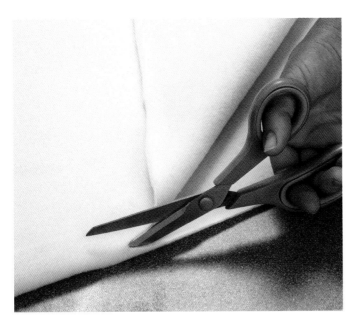

STEP 1 Fold the fleece in half lengthways and cut it to make two equal-sized pieces.

STEP 2 Cut off any edgings (which may be simple stitched folds or satin). Lay the two pieces on top of each other and stitch them together on three sides, ³⁄₄in/20mm in from the edge.

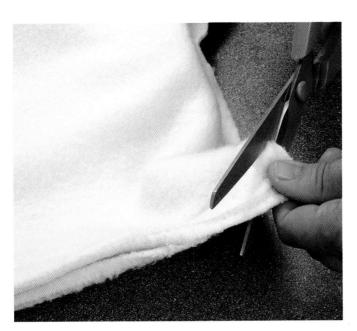

STEP 3 Snip across the corners, then turn the other way out to conceal the seams and press flat, using a damp cloth to protect the fleece surface from the direct heat.

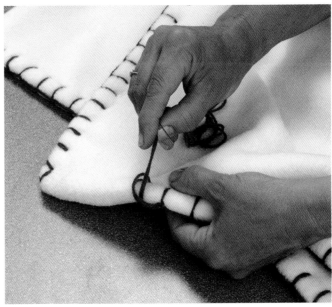

STEP 4 Thread the large needle with tapestry wool and sew a large blanket stitch on the three closed sides. Put the cushion pad inside and slip-stitch to close the open end. Continue the blanket stitch along this seam.

YOU WILL NEED:

• **FOAM CUBE,**
  18IN/460MM SQUARE

• **FABRIC**

• **SCISSORS**

• **TAPE MEASURE**

• **T-PINS**

• **IRON**

• **SEWING MACHINE**

• **NEEDLE AND THREAD**

PROJECT TWO
Cube seat

A smart, fabric-covered foam cube is great for spare seating, and can double as a side table. Have an 18in/460mm square of foam cut to size professionally, and use medium-to-heavyweight fabric; avoid stretchy fabrics, because they will sag and the cover must be taut.

The fabric for covering the base does not have to match the main fabric, because it will not be seen, but it should be hardwearing. A neutral-colored, textured fabric has been used here, in contrast to the graphic straight lines of the cube. Take a ⅝in/15mm seam allowance throughout.

If you want to use the cube permanently as a side table, place an 18in/460mm square of hardboard inside to rest on top of the foam, then slip the cover on top.

HOW TO DO IT

STEP 1 Cut a 19¼in/490mm square of fabric for the cube top, and four rectangles 19⅝in/500mm for the side panels. With the right sides facing, stitch the side panels together along the long edges, starting ⅝in/15mm below the upper edge. Press the seams open.

STEP 2 With the right sides facing, stitch the sides to the top, matching the seams to the corners. Pivot the fabric at the corners, then clip the corners. Press the seam toward the side panels.

STEP 3 Cut an 18⅜in/470mm square of fabric to cover the base. Press ⅝in/15mm under on the outer edges.

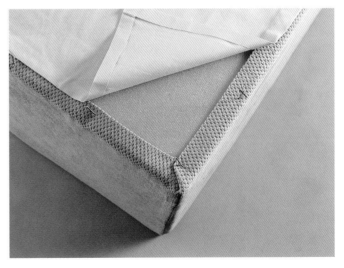

STEP 4 Slip the cover over the foam, positioning the seams at the edges. Pin the raw edges to the base of the foam with upholstery T-pins, folding under the fullness at the corners. Pin the base cover centrally on top. Slipstitch to the base with a double length of thread.

YOU WILL NEED:

- DUPION SILK
- ORGANZA
- AIR-ERASABLE PEN
- SEWING MACHINE OR
  NEEDLE AND THREAD
- IRON
- PINKING SHEARS
- 2 TASSELS

PROJECT THREE

Tasselled table runner

Create an air of sophistication at a dinner party with a silk table runner edged in sparkling organza. A silver tassel sewn to each point emphasizes the metallic threads in the organza and hangs elegantly off each end of the table.

TIP
To avoid a noticeable ridge around the edge of the silk caused by pressing, after you have pressed the seam towards the runner, run the tip of the iron around the edge of the runner under the seam allowance.

HOW TO DO IT

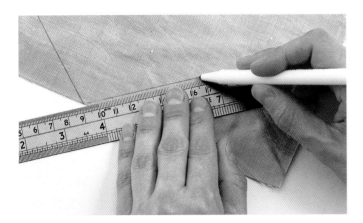

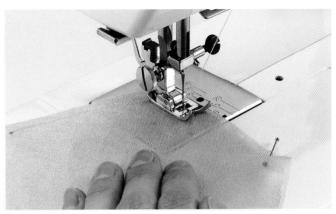

STEP 1 Cut a strip of dupion silk 42¹/₂in x 10⁵/₈in/1077mm x 270mm for the runner (allow ³/₈in/10mm seam), and cut two strips of organza for the side borders 37⁵/₈ x 5¹/₂in/950 x 140mm. Refer to the diagrams to cut the ends to points. Use the pattern to cut four end borders from organza. It would be best to redraw the pattern to actual size.

STEP 2 Trace the two dots onto the end borders with an air-erasable pen. With right sides facing, stitch the end borders together in pairs along the notched ends between the dots. Trim the seam allowance to ¹/₄in/6mm. Clip the corners and press the seams open. Finger-press the seams at the points that are difficult to reach with the tip of the iron.

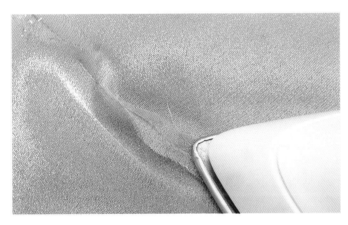

STEP 3 With the right sides facing, stitch the end borders between the side borders, inside the dots. Clip the corners and press the seams open. Trim the seam allowance to ¹/₄in/6mm. Press the border in half with the wrong sides facing, matching the seams and raw edges. Machine-tack the raw edges together.

STEP 4 With the right sides facing, pin the border to the runner, matching the seams to the corners. Stitch in place, pivoting the stitching at the dots. Neaten the seam with a zigzag stitch or pinking shears, and press the seam toward the runner. Sew a tassel to the pointed tips of the runner.

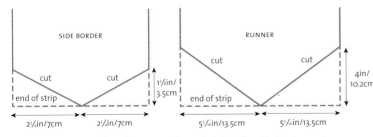

These two diagrams show how to cut the material for the side borders and the runner, as described in Step 1.

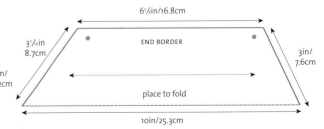

This diagram shows how to cut the material for the four end borders, as described in Step 1.

YOU WILL NEED:

- Toile de Jouy fabric
- plain fabric
- Scissors
- thin card pen
- tailor's chalk
- 2oz/56g wadding, 13ft/4m x 3ft/915mm
- long ruler
- curved basting pins

PROJECT FOUR
Scalloped quilt

This pretty, scallop-edged quilt is reversible, with a classic Toile de Jouy fabric on one side and a muted plain fabric on the other. The quilt measures 6ft 4in x 4ft 9in/1950mm x 1450mm, and can thus be made from 5ft/1525mm wide fabric.

If you are using a narrower width fabric, join the widths with flat seams, with the full width along the centre and an equal amount at each side. Remember to allow extra fabric to match patterns. Sew the widths together before drawing the scallops.

This quilt is delightfully feminine. Make it the focal point of the bedroom and pick out the colors on the walls and other soft furnishings.

HOW TO DO IT

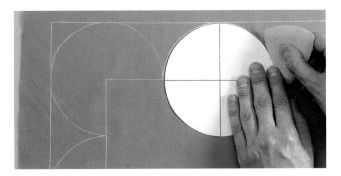

STEP 1 Cut a 4³⁄₄in/120mm diameter circle of thin card for a template for the scallops. Divide the circle into fourths with a pen. Lay the plain fabric out flat, wrong side face up. With tailor's chalk, draw a 6ft 4in x 4ft 9in/1950mm x 1450mm rectangle on the plain fabric. Draw a 2³⁄₈in/60mm deep margin inside the rectangle. Place the circle template on one corner, matching the fourth lines to the inner corner of the margin. Draw around three-fourths of the circle on the margin. Repeat on each corner. Move the template along the inner edges of the margin and draw a row of semicircles edge to edge for the scallops.

STEP 2 Cut 13ft/4m of 3ft/915mm wide 2oz/56g wadding widthways in half. Butt the long edges together and join with a herringbone stitch. Place the printed fabric on top with the right side face up, smoothing the layers outward from the center.

STEP 3 With the right sides facing, place the plain fabric wrong side up on the printed fabric. Smooth the layers outward from the center and tack or pin together with curved basting pins. Stitch along the scallops, leaving a 20in/510mm gap to turn.

STEP 4 On the right side of the printed fabric, mark the position of the unstitched scallops with tailor's chalk. Stitch along the drawn lines to secure the wadding to the fabric, taking care not to catch in the plain fabric.

STEP 5 Carefully trim away the wadding in the seam allowance close to the stitching. Trim the seam allowance to ¼in/6mm. Snip the curves and corners. Turn right side out and gently press the edges of the scallops so the wadding is not squashed flat. Turn the raw edges to the inside and slipstitch together.

STEP 6 Tack the layers together or pin with curved basting pins. Lay the quilt out flat, printed side face up. Use a long ruler and tailor's chalk to draw straight lines along the length between the inner corners of the scallops. Starting on a center line, stitch along the lines with the sewing machine set to a long stitch length.

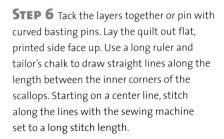

YOU WILL NEED:
- ARTIST'S CANVAS TO SIZE
- DESIGN REFERENCE
- RULER
- SET SQUARE
- PENCIL
- SCISSORS
- COMBINATION SQUARE
- STRAIGHT EDGE
- DOUBLE-SIDED CARPET TAPE
- IRON
- PAINTER'S TAPE
- ACRYLIC PRIME
- 2IN/50MM BRUSH
- NUMBER 6 FLAT BRUSH
- COLORED LATEX MATCH POTS
- ROUND ARTIST'S BRUSHES
- MAT VARNISH

PROJECT FIVE

Floor cloth: painting canvas

Hand-painted, individually designed canvas floor coverings owe their origins to the early New World pioneers, who reputedly re-used their boat sails as the raw material.

The design used on this canvas depicts an historical American theme, based on colors and shapes used by native peoples of the Southwest desert states.

HOW TO DO IT

STEP 1 "Square up" the raw canvas, leaving a 2in/50mm border to be folded over, and cut the corners diagonally.

STEP 2 Fold the border to conceal the rough edges, and iron in the crease after damping down the canvas.

STEP 3 Use double-sided carpet tape (available from hardware stores) to secure the folded border permanently in position.

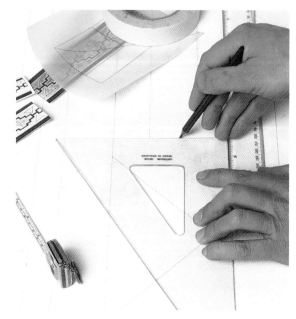

STEP 4 Some canvas is sold preprimed, some raw. If you buy yours raw, give it a coat of white acrylic primer.

STEP 5 Pencil your geometric design onto the canvas, using set square, measure, and straight edge to keep it symmetrical.

STEP 6 Painting: use a number o artist's brush to fill in the corners.

STEP 7 Use painter's tape to achieve an accurate, straight side stripe.

STEP 8 Use brown paper to protect the finished areas as you work.

Little Details

Some people would say that it is the smallest details of design in a house that really turn it into a home. In this chapter we explore some smaller projects that could add the finishing touches to a room. First we discover that it is possible to personalize a vase with a simple paint job. Then, basic tiling skills are called for to help you make a mosaic mirror frame in a Moorish style, which you could combine with the Moorish-style lantern also described in the following pages. We show how a basic lampshade and base can be transformed to match in with the theme of a room or to stand out as a particularly attractive feature, using buttons or shells. One of the most important ways of adding personal style to a room is through the display of photographs, and we offer a project to make a delightful and stylish padded photo frame. These projects all show that the little things in life can mean a great deal in the world of home decoration.

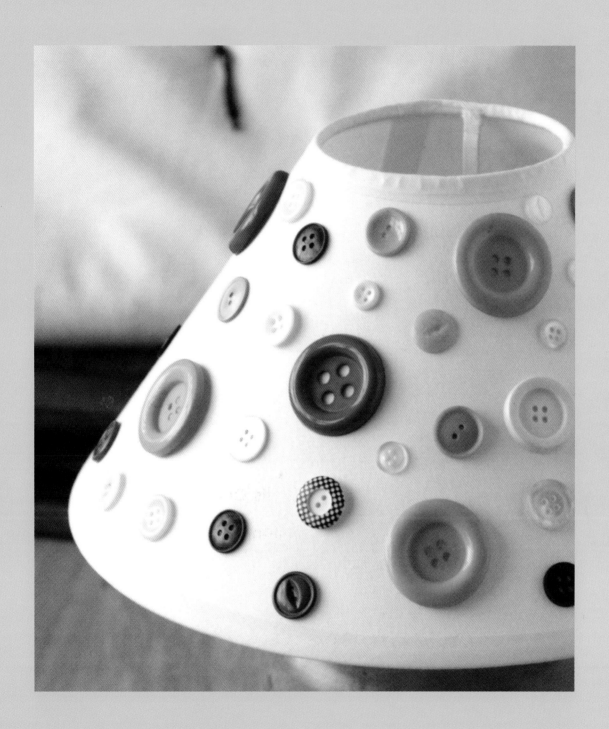

YOU WILL NEED:
- TRANSPARENT SELF-ADHESIVE PLASTIC FILM
- PENCIL
- SCISSORS OR CRAFT KNIFE
- NATURAL SPONGE
- RANGE OF COLORS OF CERAMIC PAINTS
- ARTIST'S BRUSHES

PROJECT ONE

Painting vases

Enliven a plain vase by decorating it with ceramic paints, available from arts and crafts suppliers. Decant the paint into a small kettle or pot and sponge on tint combinations of the same color, or be more adventurous and mask out an area for hand-painting a foreground design.

HOW TO DO IT

STEP 1 Draw a sunflower head on self-adhesive plastic film and carefully cut out as a mask.

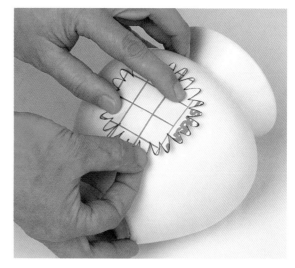

STEP 2 Hold the mask up to the vase to check the size and the position and then stick it on.

STEP 3 Using a natural sea sponge, put on the first tint of the color.

STEP 4 Sponge on the second tint, to start the build-up of the broken color effect.

STEP 5 Now add the third, darker shade; this gives a three-dimensional feel to the design.

STEP 6 Peel off the sunflower head mask and the vase is ready for hand-painting.

STEP 7 Paint in bright yellow petals using a number 5 artist's brush. The shadow detail in orange will require a thinner brush.

STEP 8 On a mid-brown base, touch in the minute black detail in the sunflower center with a number 1 brush.

YOU WILL NEED:
- ¹⁄₂IN/12MM
  PLYWOOD BASE 16IN
  x 10IN/400MM
  x 250MM
- ¹⁄₂IN/12MM
  PLYWOOD FRAME
  PIECES, 2 x 2IN x
  14IN/50MM x
  350MM AND 2 x 2IN
  x 8IN/50MM x
  200MM
- MIRROR, CUT TO SIZE
- WOOD GLUE AND
  CLAMPS
- TILE ADHESIVE AND
  TERRA COTTA-TINTED
  GROUT
- MOSAIC TESSERAE
- MOSAIC SNIPPERS
- WHITE GLUE
- BRUSH
- MIRROR FIXINGS
  AND SCREWS

PROJECT TWO
Mosaic mirror frame

Tiling is very much a part of the Moorish style, and a mirror framed with tiles will look perfect in a room with a Moorish theme. If you have never made a mosaic before, then this is the project to start with. Mosaic is not difficult, and there is always a wonderful surprise at the end when the grouting is wiped off and the bright jewel colors are revealed. You could choose mosaic tesserae in colors that would appear in Moroccan tiling such as blue, white, orange and black, and either adapt an existing frame or make a new one one from plywood. A cut-down border of tiles around the inside edge of the mirror creates the illusion of depth.

Learning how to make mosaics is quite straightforward and is very rewarding.

HOW TO DO IT

Begin by making a simple plywood backing with a wide frame stuck on it as a recess for a mirror. Make the frame the width of three or four layers of tesserae, then you will not need to trim any of the pieces.

STEP 1 Begin by making a simple plywood backing with a wide frame stuck on it as a recess for a mirror. Lay out the pattern before gluing to get the effect you want.

STEP 2 Glue each piece in place . This is a very simple pattern and you should not need to trim any of the pieces.

STEP 3 When the frame pattern is laid, glue the mirror into the middle with a lot of glue.

STEP 4 You may need to cut tiles to fit into the area between the mirror and the surface of the mosaic. Glue uncut tesserae to the outside edge of the frame so that they align with the surface of the mosaic. Grout the mosaic, making sure that the grout fills all the gaps, then polish the tiles and mirror with a soft cloth.

YOU WILL NEED:
• A SELECTION OF
  BUTTONS
• TUBE OF CLEAR GLUE
• LAMPSHADE

PROJECT THREE

Lampshades

It is often difficult to find a lampshade to match the color scheme of your room, but there is no need to worry because lampshades can be painted with ordinary latex paint, and a test pot of color will be enough to transform two medium-sized shades or one large one. Plain colors look great, but patterns can be stamped or stenciled on, and you can also add trimmings such as a fringe, baubles, or beads in contrasting or harmonizing colors. The lampshade in the project is embellished with buttons stuck on with clear glue. Before the throwaway culture took over, every home had a button tin, and nowadays these often turn up at flea markets and thrift shops. Old buttons can be really beautiful, and even the plain shell or mother-of-pearl types are well worth showing off on a lampshade or cushion cover.

Bases of lamps can be decorated as well as the shades. This seaside-style lamp base has been given a wet sand effect with shells attached using strong glue.

HOW TO DO IT

STEP 1 Plan the arrangement of the buttons on the shade. Apply a blob of glue to each.

STEP 2 Hold each button firmly against the shade until you feel the glue bonding. Continue with this until you have used all your chosen buttons.

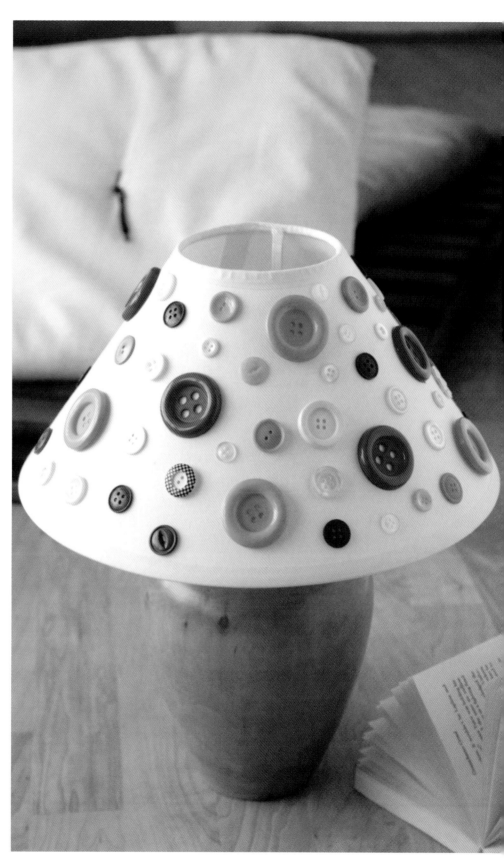

YOU WILL NEED:
• FABRIC
• SCISSORS
• IRON
• BEADS
• LAMPSHADE RING

PROJECT FOUR
Lanterns

Lend an exotic feel to a room with a flamboyant fabric lantern. Ideally suited to Eastern style decor, lanterns are inexpensive to create and can be embellished with beads and tassels. Instead of a lampshade frame, the lantern is supported by a utility lampshade ring, which is available from craft suppliers.

This shapely lantern is particularly effective if it is made from shot silk, because it will subtly change color when viewed from different angles. Beads are sewn to the points in the lantern made here, but you could attach tassels instead if you prefer. It is important to take ⅜in/1cm seam allowances throughout.

Add an exotic touch to a bedroom or living room with this unusually shaped lantern.

HOW TO DO IT

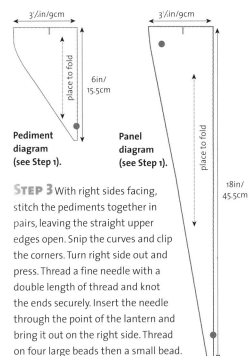

3¹/₂in/9cm

place to fold

6in/15.5cm

Pediment diagram (see Step 1).

3¹/₂in/9cm

place to fold

18in/45.5cm

Panel diagram (see Step 1).

³/₈in/1cm

STEP 1 From fabric, cut six panels and six pediments. Taking a ³/₈in/1cm seam allowance, stitch the panels together in pairs along one long edge, ending the stitching at the lower dot.

STEP 2 Stitch all the panels together along the long edges, stitching two opposite seams between the dots for attaching to the lampshade ring. Press each seam open after stitching. Trim the seam allowance to ¹/₄in/5mm at the lower edge and point to reduce the bulk. Turn the lantern right side out.

STEP 3 With right sides facing, stitch the pediments together in pairs, leaving the straight upper edges open. Snip the curves and clip the corners. Turn right side out and press. Thread a fine needle with a double length of thread and knot the ends securely. Insert the needle through the point of the lantern and bring it out on the right side. Thread on four large beads then a small bead.

STEP 4 Pull the beads along the thread so the first large bead is against the lantern point. Insert the needle back up through the large beads to the inside of the lantern so the small bead rests on the last large bead. Repeat to fix the beads securely. Sew one large bead and a small bead to the point of each pediment. Tack the raw edges together.

STEP 5 With the right side of the pediments facing the wrong side of the lantern, stitch each pediment to a lantern panel, matching the notches. Press the seams open.

STEP 6 Slip the lantern through a 12in/30cm diameter utility lampshade ring. Lift each pediment over the ring, positioning the seams with a ³/₈in/1cm gap at the intersections of the ring.

STEP 7 Slipstitch the top of the pediments together edge to edge for ³/₈in/1cm. Catch to the panel seams with a few stitches, enclosing the ring.

YOU WILL NEED:

- **THICK CARD**
- **SCISSORS**
- **AIR-ERASABLE PEN**
- **4oz/112G WADDING**
- **VELVET FABRIC**
- **COTTON FACING FABRIC**
- **FABRIC GLUE**
- **CRAFT KNIFE**

PROJECT FIVE

Padded photo frame

A treasured photograph needs a special setting. A padded photo frame is very effective and would make a delightful gift. Adapt the technique to make frames to your personal requirements by altering the shape and size. Although velvet can be difficult to sew, only a small amount of stitching is involved in covering the frame.

Velvet is a perfect fabric for this photo frame, but other fabrics work very well, too—try gingham or chintz.

HOW TO DO IT

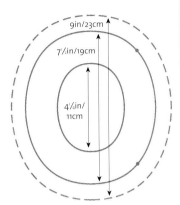

Template for photo frame,
as described in Steps 1 and 2.

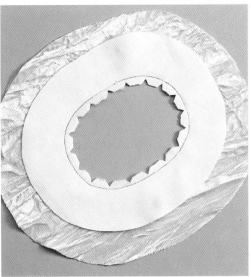

STEP 1 Draw a template (see left). Cut two frames from card and one from wadding. Cut out the window on one card frame. Stick the wadding to this frame. Cut two frames from velvet: don't cut out the window. Cut a facing from cotton, cutting ¼in/5mm inside the outer solid line. Draw the window on it. Right sides together, pin the facing to a velvet frame; stitch along the window outline. Cut out the window, leaving a ¼in/5mm seam allowance. Snip the curves. Press the facing to the inside.

STEP 2 Place front frame wadding-side down on the velvet frame. Move the seam allowance to underside of front frame. Pull facing through to back. Glue facing to underside of frame. Pull outer edges smoothly over underside and stick. Cover remaining card frame with remaining velvet frame, gluing raw edges onto the underside. Wrong sides facing, slipstitch frames together along the outer edges, leaving a gap at one side between the dots to insert your photograph.

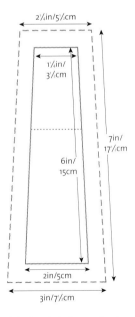

Template for photo frame stand,
as described in Steps 3 and 4.

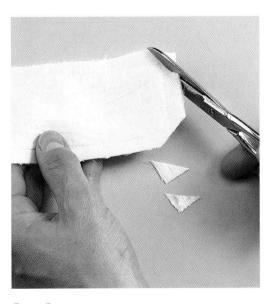

STEP 3 Cut two stands from velvet, cutting along the broken lines. Press under ⅜in/1cm along the lower wide ends. With right sides facing, stitch the stands together along the raw edges, taking ⅜in/1cm seam allowance, leaving the lower edge open. Clip the corners and turn through.

STEP 4 Cut a stand from thick card, cutting along the solid lines. Score across the dotted lines on the card stand with a craft knife. Bend the stand outward along the scored line. Insert the card stand into the velvet stand. Slipstitch the lower edge closed. Glue the upper 1½in/4cm of the stand to the back of the frame.

Index